Any More for Sailing?

A Personal Look at Bridlington Harbour

Mike Wilson

1996

DEDICATION

This book is dedicated to all Bridlington families who have husbands, fathers, sons or brothers at work on the sea.

It is also dedicated, with affectionate memory, to all those Bridlington people who participated in "Come Hell or High Water," the Bridlington Community Play, in 1995.

ACKNOWLEDGEMENTS

The author acknowledges the assistance of many people during the compilation of this book.

He also acknowledges the following sources of information: Pleasure Steamers of Old Yorkshire, by Arthur Godfrey; The Bridlington Book, by Bryan Waites; The Bridlington Lifeboats, by Ralph S. Fawcett; Bridlington, 50 Years a Borough; Welcome to Bridlington Harbour, Bridlington Harbour Commissioners; The Three Brothers, The Bridlington Sailing Coble Preservation Society; Fishing Vessels of Britain & Northern Ireland; the Royal Yorkshire Yacht Club 1847-1947; Olsen's Fisherman's Nautical Almanack; the Bridlington Free Press; the staff in Bridlington Library for the Bridlington Room; and many other individuals whose lives are ruled by the sea.

"Any More for Sailing?"
photographed, written and designed by Mike Wilson, and typeset by him at The Print Shop, 44 Quay Road, Bridlington YO15 2AP, with thanks to Barry.
Printed by Wards Printers (Bridlington) Ltd., 55 West Street, Bridlington YO15 3DX.
Published by Prestyme Publications, 44 Quay Road, Bridlington YO15 2AP.

ISBN 0 952814 0 05

ABOUT THE AUTHOR

Mike Wilson is a Bridlingtonian who spent his childhood in the town before commencing an apprenticeship with the Bridlington Chronicle until it merged with the Bridlington Free Press in 1954. National Service followed completion of his printing training and then he returned to East Yorkshire for a short time to work with East Yorkshire Printers at Driffield. Seeking wider experience, he moved to Maidenhead into magazine production and then to Aylesbury where he joined the local newspaper. Ten years later he returned to Bridlington and East Yorkshire Newspapers where he became production manager. A partnership preceded Mike's own business, QuickSilver Typesetters, and this was followed by a working period on local newspapers which ended in March 1994. He is now managing The Print Shop, Bridlington.

Mike's interest in publishing started when he produced a tenpin bowling newspaper and locally he has produced The First Bridlington Fun & Quiz Book and A Postcard from Bridlington.

Mike is married to Ann and they have three children, Guy, Lynne and Paul.

In his leisure time, Mike is a prize-winning member of Bridlington Writers' Group, enjoys photography and is a keen tenpin bowler.

He played Kit Brown in the Bridlington Community Play "Come Hell or High Water" in 1995.

CONTENTS

387.150

HARBOUR STATISTICS

North Pier	
Length	670ft.
Width	25-30ft.
South Pier	
Length	1520ft.
Width	15ft.
Chicken Run	
Length	442ft.
Width	15ft.
Crane Wharf Pier	
Length	214ft.
Width	30ft.
Harbour entrance	90ft. wide
Enclosed area	11.5 acres
Tidal range	Nil to 27ft.
Crane	SWL 7-ton on South Pier
Quayage for fishing craft	225ft. approx.
Permitted berths	39 trawlers
	17 commercial cobles
	29 angling cobles
Chart Ref.	54deg 5min North
	0deg 12min West
Flags/Lights	Red more than 9ft. water
	Green less than 9ft. water
Storm Cones	▲ Northerly gale
	▼ Southerly gale
Harbour Master	W. J. Mason

Harbour Authorities:
Bridlington Harbour Commissioners
Harbour Road, Bridlington. Tel. (01262) 678302

Bridlington Harbour – a brief history

The shelter provided by Flamborough Head and the protection afforded by the Gypsey Race has given seafarers a place to moor in times of storm. It is thought that trade routes in prehistoric times terminated in this area before settlements arose.

Evidence of Roman life has been excavated in Bridlington Quay and since then the Harbour has gradually evolved into the thriving place of business and pleasure it is now.

Before Roman times and since, fishing has played an important part of life for the people in Bridlington Quay although the Harbour has also been used by other traders.

In early records it is shown that the ownership of the Harbour was transferred from Gilbert de Gant to the Priory of Bridlington. This took place in 1113 after the founding of the monastery. King Stephen issued a mandate to "permit The Prior of Bridlington to have, hold well and in peace, the Harbour of Bridlington." Until the era of Henry VIII, the Priory had the right to collect tolls, but, at the Dissolution, the Manor and Harbour came under the King's power.

Its early use as a port was for trade in timber, grain, ale and agricultural products, but wool was the most profitable trade in the 14th century, and Bridlington Priory was among the top wool producing monasteries. Smuggling was also evident in those days and *La Mariole*, the monastery's own boat, was involved, but the prior of 1339, Robert de Scardebergh, was acquitted of the offence.

On the orders of the King, a local ship was seized for use in the French War, and it is said a Bridlington ship carried soldiers to the battle of Crecy in 1343. In 1401 Henry IV commanded the bailiffs of Bridlington to transport food to troops in Scotland in a locally built boat.

King Henry VIII took over the Harbour in

Two aerial views of Bridlington harbour, the first showing the harbour from the landward end of South Pier, the other looking into the harbour mouth from a point over the sea. Note in the earlier photo, above, taken in the 20s, there is no covered accommodation for the fishing activities. On the newer picture, post-1933 as the Victoria Rooms have disappeared from the scene, *Yorkshireman* is alongside North Pier and two large freighters are unloading on South Pier.

1537, and a rebuilding programme was soon under way. Stone from the destroyed Priory and labour from tenants in the town and surrounding villages was used. The piers were of wood, broad based narrowing to a decking along the top. The main timber frames were divided into sections which were filled with stone. The weakest point was where the pier joined the land and breaches by the sea, followed by expensive rebuilding, occurred in 1537, 1562, 1579, 1591, 1643, 1664, 1697 and 1717.

In 1550 a survey by Dalton and Bethell found that the piers were decaying but there was no timber for repairs, and one townsman was imprisoned when no books or records had been kept.

Lack of money over the next 200 years meant that the Harbour was always in poor condition when frequent storms broke the wooden piers.

Trade continued, with malt and grain being exported while coal was imported. This trade did suffer, however, through Dutch pirates in 1660. The town was protected by two forts but naval protection was non-existent.

Perhaps the most famous incident of the Harbour's chequered history occurred on 23rd February, 1643, when Queen Henrietta Maria arrived at Bridlington Harbour. She was on her way to Newcastle having pledged personal jewellery to buy arms for Charles I's cause in the Civil War. However, a storm forced her into the Bay. After two days at anchor, her ships entered the Harbour, and the Queen took shelter near Queen Street. Parliament ships bombarded the

Above: Before the erection of Ebor Flats and the building of the restaurant/hotel complex.
Centre: A view of Bridlington Quay in the days of sail.
Bottom: A harbour scene during the 30s, with *Yorkshireman* and *Thornwick*.

Quay and the Queen was forced to take refuge on the banks of the Gypsey Race. The arms and ammunition were loaded onto 500 carts and were dispatched to York on 8th March, 1643.

Robert Fowler, a Quaker, built a ship near the Harbour about 1657 and sailed for America. Although neither he nor his companions knew anything about navigation, they reached America close to their intended destination.

In the 18th century, the building of ships flourished with the largest being the *Albion*, a 325-ton whaler. In the early nineteenth century, several shipbuilding businesses were present in the town, and brigs of about 230 tons were built. The Napoleonic wars saw them armed, as was the *Guardian*, 230 tons and with six six-pounders, built for trade with the Cape of Good Hope. *The Queen Dowager* was Bridlington's last ship, built in 1843 by Nelson Hewitt. Local ships sailed to English and European ports and even to the Arctic, having a reputation for being well built.

Six local ships were still trading from the Harbour in 1862, three in 1872, while the last coal ship continued until the end of the century. The last import of potash took place in 1974.

The old South Pier was where the current Chicken Run is situated, and until about 1820 the Harbour was half today's size. John Rennie, a famous engineer, was appointed to survey the Harbour and its expansion and by 1816 work had begun. By 1848 both piers had been built, the North Pier costing £80,000 and taking 23 years to build. The South Pier cost considerably less, £40,000 and five years. However, due to the arrival of the railways in the town in 1846, port trade slumped and the Quay's future was undecided.

In 1846, 825 ships entered the harbour, not including fishing boats.

A 120ft. extension to the North Pier in 1866 at a cost of £6,000 was planned by J. Coode, of York, and this gave added protection, gaining for Bridlington the advantage of being a Harbour of Refuge.

Fishing was to continue of course and, as Bridlington became a known resort, pleasure sailing commenced with some 30 yawls being available in 1885.

The original Chicken Run built in 1904 was of timber and 6ft wide. The present construction, built in 1950/51, has a concrete deck.

By 1900 some 40 sailing cobles operated for fishing trips and some of these are still present, although now motorised. Pleasure steamers arrived with *Frenchman*, then

Above: The oldest part of Bridlington harbour, Clough Hole. The Gypsey Race flows into the harbour at this point.

Below: Old sailors and their families seen collecting water from the spring pump at the harbour side. A plaque regarding its discovery can be seen at the bottom of Slipway Hill.

Yorkshireman, while today there is the *Yorkshire Belle* and *Flamborian*.

An annual attraction before the second world war was the Regatta and Aquatic Sports, while there have been frequent visits from Royal Navy vessels since the first world war.

From about 1928 the Royal Air Force had a presence in the Harbour with their air sea rescue unit. They were situated on Gummers Landing, built by Dobb and Gummer of Rotherham in 1885 and first used as a fish wharf, but later boats were hauled out of the water there for repair. The building is now the Lawrence Complex.

The end of the South Pier was widened in the early 1930s to form a covered fish wharf and accommodation, and more improvements followed in 1950. The present building, opened on 10th June 1975 by Lord Halifax, provides modern facilities for the fishing industry and some time later an ice-making machine was installed.

Other more recent developments have included the building of the walkway from Harbour Road to the landward end of the Chicken Run and South Pier. The footbridge was erected in 1968-69 and other improvements carried out. The bridge was found to be potentially dangerous and was dismantled in early 1996.

Langdale Wharf has been changed into a car park alongside which new fishermen's sheds have been built. The latest modernisation has taken place at Crane Wharf with the addition of several new shops. The shops on street level are close to the location of the former Cliff Terrace, the home of Captain George Symons, R.A., winner of a Victoria Cross before Sebastopol in 1855.

Dominating the Harbour just here for nearly a hundred years were the Victoria Rooms. Built in 1846, the building included a ballroom, billiard room, news room and reading room. In 1879 it was bought by the local Government Board. The last meeting of the Town Council was held on 9th November 1899. The building itself was destroyed by fire on 22nd September 1933.

The Great Gale

The story has been told many times. But like all good stories it bears repeating. The Great Gale of 10th February 1871 is one of the memorable times of Bridlington's history. Great bravery, great commitment, great sacrifice: all were there.

Having become becalmed the previous day, hundreds of sailing ships faced gradually increasing wind strength. Sleet and snow came with gales from the south-east, the worst scenario for Bridlington Bay.

Some vessels were deliberately run ashore in an attempt to beat the storm. Other masters decided to stay at sea. Eventually, the storm worsened to such an extent that anchors were dragged and vessels were forced ashore. The ships were in poor condition and broke up quickly. Many sailors died in the savage sea's arms within sight, hearing and often arm's length of onlookers.

Coastguards and the rocket services were stretched to the limit and the lifeboats did magnificent service.

The national lifeboat, the *Robert Whitworth*, and the fishermen's boat, the *Harbinger*, fought the mountainous seas to rescue many sailors in distress. *Robert Whitworth* saved the crews of the *Echo* and the *Windsor*, and the crew battled for many hours until they were exhausted. This vessel was eventually taken off duty as it was too unwieldy and heavy for the conditions, but she had saved 12 men.

The fishermen's boat, the *Harbinger*, went out time and time again, making several rescues.

After seven trips into the terrible seas, her crew was rested and a call went out for other men. David Purdon, the boat's builder, and his assistant John Clappison, volunteered.

The crew pulled through the breakers and went to the aid of the *Delta* of Whitby. All but one of the crew had perished and a lone seaman was clutching the rigging at the stern.

As the lifeboat pulled closer to the *Delta*, the man refused to jump. Then a huge wave upturned the lifeboat. The crew of nine were thrown into the water but three of them, John Robinson, Robert Hopper and Richard Bedlington, hung onto the boat. They drifted ashore helpless in the vessel.

Those that were lost were Richard Atkin, John Clappison, William Cobb, Robert Pickering, David Purdon and James Watson, and a monument to their sacrifice stands in the churchyard of the Priory.

It was estimated that over 40 seamen lost their lives that dreadful day and many vessels sunk. After the storm had subsided, wreckage of all kinds was piled high at the foot of Bridlington's sea walls.

For many years, a service was held in the Priory Church for those who perished but this has evolved into a Lifeboat Service.

In early 1995, the Bridlington Town Play, "Come Hell or High Water," re-enacted the events of that day and its aftermath.

BRIDLINGTON HARBOUR MASTERS

1755	Roger Bielby	Died
1755 to 1779	John Ellis	Died
1779 to 1808	Francis Ellis	Died
1808 to 1828	John Belland	Resigned
1828 to 1839	William Nelson Howard	Discharged
1839 to 1841	Francis Catley	Resigned
1841 to 1843	Benjamin Lamplugh	Resigned
1843 to 1845	Francis Cobb	Died
1845 to 1873	John Campleman	Died
1873 to 1896	John Gray	Resigned
1896 to 1906	Albert Robert Stephenson	Died
1906 to 1924	Thomas Henry Jackson	Resigned
1924 to 1928	William Seager	Died
1928 to 1960	Lieutenant Edward Taylor	Retired
1960 to 1974	Captain Rowland Spear	Retired
1974 to 1991	George Wallis	Retired
1991 to 1993	Phil Thornton	Resigned
1993	Terry Dealtry	Resigned
1993 to date	W. J. Mason	

Remember those who have to
  sail
And are off their courses
  blown.
When the gales of winter
  throw their might
At Bridlington's harbour stone.

Acknowledge the bravery of
  those men
And watch with eyes appalled.
Listen for the rocket's boom
As out the lifeboat's called.

The seas are just as fierce now
As in 1871,
When *Harbinger* died and
  crewmen too,
Six lives given, nothing won.

So spare a coin, or note or
  cheque
For the national lifeboatmen
And support those saviours o
  the sea,
Don't let them die in vain.

Top and bottom:
Views of the
harbour from a
distance; right:
The fish dock;
below right:
Harbourmaster's
Office and
Museum; below:
The weathervane
on north pier.

Yorkshire Belle

48 years old and still cruising

The *Yorkshire Belle*, built to replace the *Royal Jubilee* which was transferred to Falmouth, was launched at Messrs Cook, Welton and Gemmell's Beverley yard by Miss L. Twidle, daughter of the managing director of the shipyard. She was built for A. and W. Crawford. She was over 24m overall with a 5m beam and a draught of just over a metre. She had twin 88hp Kelvin diesel engines which gave a speed of 10 knots. There was a saloon bar, a ladies' cabin and she could carry 200 passengers. Board of Trade tests were carried out before the vessel sailed to Bridlington.

The local newspaper reported that the *Yorkshire Belle*, Bridlington's sixth and latest cruiser, arrived on Thursday, 19th May, 1938. It was the first time she had been at sea, as her trials were conducted on the Humber. The journey from Hull was made with 40 passengers on board. Her saloon was finished in mahogany and chromium plate, the vessel was painted white and the seating was of leather cushions. She had a cruiser stern and the latest streamlined bows, and everything was controlled from the bridge. Mr Jack Pockley was the skipper and she was to operate from the North Pier, as she was too large to operate from the wooden steps.

This vessel was destroyed during the war when she hit a magnetic mine in the Humber and was lost with all hands.

A replacement *Yorkshire Belle* was built in 1947 also by Cook, Welton & Gemmell, No. 793, with a length of over 24m, a breadth of nearly six metres and a depth of 1.7m. She weighs 70 tons gross. Two eight-cylinder Gardner engines each give 152hp and she can carry up 212 passengers. She is fully licensed with a lounge bar and ladies' saloon, and light refreshments are served on the cruises.

There is a public commentary pointing out items of local interest along Flamborough Head, and to add to the pleasure there is a souvenir shop and live music is played.

As well as relaxing one-hour cruises to Flamborough Head, there are special long cruises to Bempton Bird Sanctuary with close-up views of the cliffs, lighthouse and caves.

She was bought in 1982 by her current owners, Mr Roy Simpson and Mr Peter Richardson.

Before the purchase both men worked in Huddersfield but have now become Board of Trade recognised skippers.

The first skipper was Mr Pockley until he retired in 1972, when he was followed by Mr Philip Thornton.

Harbour fees in 1995 for the *Yorkshire Belle* were £2130 + VAT.

Flamborian

The *Flamborian*, built in 1938 as *Boys' Own*, continues to give pleasure to holiday-makers in Bridlington.

She was built in Beverley, by Cook, Welton & Gemmel Ltd., the original owners being J. Newby and Consortium. As *Flamborian* she is now owned by the Connelly family. Each year between April 1 and October 30, she carries up to 180 passengers on cruises of various times and distances around Bridlington Bay, viewing the shipping lanes, the cliffs at Flamborough Head and the seabird colony at Bempton.

When built she could carry 172 passengers and was powered by twin 88hp Kelvin diesel engines which at 750rpm gave her a speed of 10 knots. Her registered tonnage was 25.2 tons. The skipper then was J. R. Newby and the engineer Mr W. Newby.

The vessel underwent Board of Trade trials in the Humber and was tested three times over a measured mile, twice against the tide and once with it. The average speed was ten knots.

She was fitted with a saloon bar and a separate ladies' cabin aft.

During the 1950s, she was structurally altered, being refitted by Mr Trevor Silverwood and renamed *Flamborian*. Her original engines were replaced with twin Gardner 6LXs at 116hp each. She has a steel riveted hull with cruiser stern and straight stem and is 21.5m overall in length, with a beam of 5.2m. She has a 1.4m draught and is nearly 1.7m out of the water.

Her fuel consumption is about six gallons per hour. Her gross tonnage is 52.22 with a registered tonnage of 27.17.

During the war the vessel saw service with R.A.S.C. on the Tees, Tyne and Humber.

She had an extensive refit over the 1986/87 winter, at both Scarborough and Grimsby.

There is a bar and toilets on board, and during cruises a running commentary is given by the crew.

In 1995, *Flamborian* cost her owners £1784 + VAT in harbour charges.

Above: *Flamborian* waits for her passengers against the north pier.

Right: *Flamborian* heads for the open sea.

Below: As *Boys' Own*, she leaves the harbour for a cruise with a large number of passengers. In the background is the twin-funnelled *Thornwick*.

Opposite, bottom: *Flamborian* makes for the harbour in evening sunshine.

Inset: *Boys' Own* enters the harbour after a cruise.

Scarborough's pleasure steamer the *Coronia* arrives at Bridlington harbour on Friday, 7th July, 1995, the first visit by a pleasure cruiser from another port for 30 years.

Scarborough's Coronia comes to town

After a period of 30 years, pleasure cruisers from Bridlington and Scarborough visited each other's port. From Bridlington, *Yorkshire Belle* made a day trip to Scarborough, while *Coronia* made the journey to Bridlington. About 80 people travelled to Scarborough while only twenty or so boarded the Coronia. In Bridlington, the *Coronia* went on an hour's cruise as did the *Belle* at Scarborough.

The day was Friday, 7th July 1995, and *Yorkshire Belle* set sail in a brisk breeze, with Peter Richardson as the skipper. Jim Eldon provided the musical entertainment.

These day trips had not been allowed due to a 15-mile limit on the *Belle*'s ordinary 'class six' licence, but extra safety equipment had brought permission from the Board of Trade. The vessel now has two reversible self-inflating liferafts each capable of carrying 65 people.

The last sailing to Scarborough by a vessel from Bridlington was in 1965 by *Thornwick*.

T.S.S. Yorkshireman

The *Yorkshireman* arrived in Bridlington harbour on Saturday, 26th May 1928, and was ready for service the following day. She had been built by Earle's Shipbuilding & Engineering Company Limited, on the Humber.

Her official number was 160 104, and main dimensions 120 x 27.1 x 8.7 feet. She had a top speed of 11.2 knots. Her power was provided two reciprocating triple expansion engines, with direct acting, vertical cylinders, of 93 n.h.p., 800 i.h.p., built by Earles Shipbuilders. She was flat-bottomed with a shallow draught to allow entrance into Bridlington Harbour and to make her useful for assisting and refloating stranded vessels.

Trials had been held the previous Thursday and had proved very satisfactory, the vessel averaging eleven and a half knots. She was larger than the *Frenchman*, then sailing from Bridlington, and could carry up to 400 passengers. There was a large lounge, a saloon forward and a ladies' saloon aft. The main saloon was panelled with polished mahogany. *Yorkshireman* was also fitted with United Towing Company's patent davits. This twin-screwed tug weighed 251 tons.

On 4th August 1928, *Yorkshireman* anchored 500 yards from the pier and 100 people enjoyed a dance from 9pm. The vessel was illuminated by hundreds of small electric lamps and the strains of dance music was easily heard on the piers and seafront.

Later that year on Monday, 28th September, *Yorkshireman* left the harbour for Hull after the end of the season. One hundred people made the journey to Hull and crowds gathered to see the vessel leave the harbour for the last time that year. A maroon was fired from the deck as a farewell signal. During the winter months, *Yorkshireman* took up towing work in the Humber.

In 1929 an agreement was made with Bridlington Harbour Commissioners and £150 was paid to cover five years harbour duties and all charges incurred for summer season excursions.

During June 1953, *Yorkshireman* towed a whale to sea which had landed on the south beach.

Except for wartime (she was requisitioned for war service on 6th October 1939) *Yorkshireman* visited the town every year, and she left Bridlington in 1954. She was towed by *Workman* to Book in Belgium where she was broken up in 1965.

Bridlington Queen

Bridlington Queen was built at East Molesley, Surrey, in 1947, and started cruising from

Bridlington that year. She was 19.6m long and weighed 26 tons. She had twin Dorman engines which were later replaced by twin Lister Blackstones. She carried 146 passengers.

*Bridlington Quee*n had an unfortunate mishap on 17th July 1966.

She had just left the harbour for her first trip of the day, when she hit a submerged rock on the canch, and soon went down by the stern. The *Queen* sank until the stern was on the bottom in about five feet of water.

Passengers stepped calmly from the *Queen* into ferryboats which had been brought out of the harbour, no-one even getting their feet wet. Mr Arthur Jenkinson, one of the owners of the speedboat *007*, towed a string of ferryboats to the *Queen* when he saw she was sinking.

Skin divers went beneath the *Queen* and

Left: *Bridlington Queen* manoeuvres in the harbour while the bottom picture shows her with a good crowd of seafarers.

used cushions from the *007* to close the hole in the ship's bottom. Pumps were then used to empty the vessel and she was towed back by the *Boys' Own*. One of the members of East Yorkshire Sub-Aqua Club, Mr Ken Ward, who provided this information, accompanied other divers who examined the vessel.

The rock was later marked then towed off to deeper water by a trawler. It was said that some of the larger boats had been operating with only a few inches clearance.

Mr Alf Wright was owner of the *Bridlington Queen* at this time.

For a period at Bridlington she had a wooden finish but she ended her time here painted white.

In the late 1980s she was on the Tay as the *Tay Queen,* before travelling to Boscombe and Newcastle.

After languishing in Cromwell Lock in Nottingham in poor condition, she was towed to Goole and scrapped during 1995.

Top picture shows the partly submerged *Bridlington Queen* with *Yorkshire Belle* in attendance.

Bottom: *Bridlington Queen* leaves the harbour as *Yorkshireman* prepares for the next cruise.

Thornwick

Thornwick arrived at Bridlington on Saturday, 26th June 1948, having been launched the previous December. She was built at Scarrs Yard in Howdendyke for Col. A. Butler of Leeds. She replaced *Royal Sovereign*, sunk during the war, and *Princess Marina*, sold to Whitby, both boats being owned by Col. Butler.

The vessel weighed 126 tons, was over 30 metres long and her top speed was 11 knots. Her specification included five watertight bulkheads. *Thornwick* could carry over 300 passengers, and was provided with a main saloon, a tea saloon and ladies' cabin over two decks.

She carried a crew of seven with Mr G. H. Colbridge (of Hull) as captain, G. Johnson (Bridlington) as skipper, and F. Johnson (bowman of Bridlington lifeboat) was the mate. G. Johnson was skipper of *Princess Marina* during 1936, 1937, 1946 and 1947. In 1953 Mr Colbridge was still captain.

Mr Ken Lester was skipper for 12 years before leaving when Mr Gordon Fox took over the *Thornwick*. Mr Jack White and Mr Arnold Woodhouse were crew members when Mr Lester was skipper.

In 1968 *Thornwick* was sold and went to Poole in Dorset where she was renamed *Swanage Queen*. She had a refit in which one of her two funnels was removed and her bridge enclosed.

It is understood that later in her life she was on the Thames at Greenwich, her accommodation covered in and being used as a restaurant.

The Royal Sovereign

The *Royal Sovereign* came to Bridlington in early May 1936, having been acquired by the local fishermen who owned the *Princess Marina*.

Built in Southend only seven years earlier, the vessel had carried up to 280 passengers from that resort. A chief feature of the vessel was the large saloon that could be used as a cafe or for dancing. The saloon contained a buffet.

The *Royal Sovereign* carried its own electric light plant (something of an innovation in those days). It was powered by two six-cylinder diesel engines developing a maximum speed of ten knots. At the front of the vessel was a cabin big enough for the crew of seven.

Royal Sovereign was fitted with two rudders. She was also fitted with wireless re-diffusion and a wireless telephone. There was a lifebelt provided for every person on a cruise.

After arrival in Bridlington, a complete renovation was carried out and the *Royal Sovereign* carried her first passengers at Whitsuntide.

The skipper of the *Princess Marina*, Mr R. E. Crawford, was to captain the new vessel, while Mr G. Johnson took over the *Princess Marina.*

The voyage from Southend to Bridlington commenced early the previous Saturday with a stop at Yarmouth to refuel. The *Royal Sovereign* behaved perfectly during the trip and was "very steady in the swells." Quite good speeds had been achieved despite the fact that the engines, which had just been overhauled, were only run at half speed.

During the war, the vessel had carried out Navy duties in the bay.

At 0206 hours on Friday, 23rd August 1940, an enemy aircraft dropped a stick of bombs over Bridlington Harbour. The first bomb struck *Royal Sovereign* and blew her to pieces.

The second bomb failed to explode, but hit a jetty and ricocheted through the bottom of *Blue Jacket*, the third bomb demolishing the Cock & Lion, Foley's Cafe and Woolworths just inland from the harbour.

The following morning on Germany's propaganda radio, Lord Haw-Haw is said to have announced the destruction of *HMS Royal Sovereign* following a raid on Bridlington by Luftwaffe bombers.

Other Pleasure Vessels of the Past

Princess Marina

On 24th April 1934, *Princess Marina*, with Mayor Cllr J. A. Drew, at the wheel, sailed into the bay. *Princess Marina* had arrived in the town six weeks earlier and was Bridlington's lastest pleasure boat. With skipper Richard E. Crawford at his side, the Mayor steered the launch into the bay for a 15-minute trip. The vessel was decorated with flags and created a great deal of interest. Formerly named *Brit*, she was owned by Mr. A. Butler, of Whitkirk, Leeds, and arrived in Bridlington from Yarmouth, where she was built by Fellows in mid-March 1928. She had sailed from South Coast resorts before coming to Bridlington and she was powered by two Kelvin engines, using paraffin. She was over 18 metres long and had a 4.5m beam. She was fireproof.

As *Brit 1*, her official number was 144157 and yard number 322. She was owned from 1928 to 1935 by E. W. & S. H. D. Longfield, running cruises from Britannia Pier and Hall Quay. In 1935 she was replaced by a vessel of the same name, being sold to Albert Butler and renamed *Princess Marina*. After being sold to Sea Cruises (Whitby) Ltd. in the period 1948 to 1952, she served the next eight years on the Thames, owned by Thorns Launches of Twickenham. From 1960 to 1976, she was owned by Alfred Crouch of London, and then sold to George Wheeler to be withdrawn from service.

Miss Mercury

In the Bridlington Free Press of 9th April 1938, it was reported that *Miss Mercury*, skippered by Mr Richard Crawford, left Goole at 8.30am on Sunday and arrived off Grimsby at 12. A very strong wind was blowing and the skipper decided to go round Spurn Point to ascertain the prevailing weather. A northerly gale was blowing and the vessel sailed three miles in a very rough sea, before returning to Grimsby.

Below: *Princess Marina* leaves the harbour for a summer cruise.

She left Grimsby on Monday at 6.30 and arrived at Bridlington at 10pm. Despite heavy seas, the boat made excellent progress. Owned by Mr Butler, of Leeds, who also owned *Royal Sovereign* and *Princess Marina*, the vessel had David Crawford Jnr as skipper and a crew of Bridlington fishermen.

She had a cruising speed of 16 knots, and was 18.4m long, with a 4.3m beam and a 0.76m draught. Her twin six-cylinder Parsons engines, each developing 125hp, made her the fastest pleasure boat in Bridlington, except for the speed boats. The engineer was Mr A. Hutchinson, also the tractor driver and chief launcher of the local lifeboat. She could carry 100 passengers and had a large saloon from the bridge to the stern. She carried a telephone from the saloon to the bridge, quite a novelty then. Built for the Thames Taxi Service, *Miss Mercury* was last used by Miss Jessie Matthews, the famous film star, who used her to travel 30 miles up the Thames every day to where the film "Sailing Along" was being made.

This vessel remains something of a mystery, as no photographic evidence has shown she was at Bridlington. Perhaps someone has a photograph of *Miss Mercury* in their collection.

Royal Jubilee

The Royal Jubilee, a twin-screw, three-cylinder Kelvin diesel-engined vessel, was built by Messrs Cook, Welton & Gemmell, of Beverley. She was the firm's No. 603 and was built in 1935. Her building provided a month's work for one hundred men. She was 22.7m long overall, and her engines produced 132hp.

Left: *Britannia* leaves the harbour with a full complement of holidaymakers. Let's hope the sun stays out!

Below: From left to right: *Royal Jubilee, May Morn* and *Princess Marina*.

She could accommodate 180-200 passengers and was equipped with a canvas awning, which covered one third of the length of the vessel, to provide covering for all passengers. The saloon, complete with buffet, could accommodate 60 people, and there was also a special cabin in the after part for thirty ladies. The fittings of the saloon were of mahogany, the decks of Borneo pine and the deck fittings of teak.

The owners were six local fishermen, who also operated the *Girls' Own* and *Britannia*. The captain was J. R. Newby, the skipper of the former boat, which was to be sold.

With a speed of 10-11 knots, *Royal Jubilee* was as fast as the *Yorkshireman*, had the latest cruiser stern, and the steering and engines could be controlled from the wheelhouse. Two fuel tanks were provided containing 140 gallons each. There was a crew of six.

Miss Twidle, daughter of Mr A. S. Twidle, J.P., of Bridlington, managing director of the builders, launched the vessel in mid-July 1935.

May Morn

No documentary evidence has been found so far regarding this vessel, although she appears in photographs.

Britannia

This vessel operated in Bridlington to at least the mid-fifties but it would be interesting to know what happened to her.

Bridlington's Paddle Steamers

Probably the first pleasure steamer seen in Bridlington Bay was a sloop-rigged paddle tug, *Transit*, built in Shields in 1848 for Leith. She was 20 metres long, built of wood and weighed 14 tons. In April, 1852, this craft came down from Scarborough but didn't enter the Harbour. The ship was owned by Jeremiah Hudson, who had charged 3/- (15p) for the trip, but the passengers would have had to pay extra to the cobles to land them in Bridlington Harbour.

Capt. Robinson's *Confidence*, built in 1862 at Middlesbrough, also visited from Scarborough the following year. Weighing 103 tons, she was a dual-purpose craft and towed Tees colliers in winter.

The London-built 36.9m paddle steamer *Scarborough* (top), much larger at 142 tons than any seen so far, was built in 1866, visiting Bridlington twice a week regularly from her namesake resort for a total of 48 years, her last trip being on 4th September 1914.

Three steam paddle boats were berthed in the town at the turn of the century: *General Havelock, Esme* and *Friends*. In 1874, *Friends* broke down near Speeton Cliffs and a small boat was sent by Master George Legg to Flamborough for help. *H.M.S. Enchantress*, an Admiralty yacht, went to *Friends'* assistance and took her in tow to Bridlington Bay.

Another popular paddle steamer at the beginning of this century was *Frenchman*, built in 1892 as *Coquet* in South Shields by J. P. Reynoldson for H. Andrews of Newcastle. She was then sold in 1899 and renamed. Owned by the United Towing Co. of Hull, she was lengthened in 1906 due her popularity but eventually scrapped in 1928

In 1899 permission was given to exhibit a board on the North Pier displaying sailing times for the *Frenchman*, but the board was forbidden on Sundays.

It is recorded that Captain Spence was in charge on 22nd July 1921, when she visited the town and that year she returned to the Humber on 7th October.

The superstructure was removed from *Frenchman* and the hull used as a dumb barge and coal hulk by United Towing at Church Lane Staith on the River Hull. She was then towed to New Holland and scrapped in 1963.

The *Bilsdale* visited the town for ten years from 1925. Built as *Lord Roberts* in Preston in 1900, this 199-ton paddle steamer carried 386 passengers. She was owned by Crosthwaite Steamship Co. of Middlesbrough and was eventually scrapped after the 1934 season.

Picture below shows both *Frenchman* and *Scarborough* alongside north pier.

One of the specialist vessels in
Bridlington Harbour

Gypsey Race

Bridlington's dredger, *Gypsey Race*, is a riveted steel vessel
capable of carrying 150 tons of spoil. She is owned by the
Bridlington Harbour Commissioners and operates not only in
the local harbour but wherever she is required. She has worked
at Amble, Berwick on Tweed, Great Yarmouth and Eyemouth.

She was built by the Renfrew firm of Lobnitz and Co. Ltd
and has a top speed of seven and a half knots from a 270hp
Volvo diesel engine.

Her dimensions are: Length 100ft, beam 25ft, loaded draft 6ft.
The crane is a Smith 2800 SWL 3.8 tonner.

Bridlington Sailing Coble Preservation Society

Among all the modern craft to be seen in Bridlington Harbour is *The Three Brothers*, a descendent of an ancient form of boat said to have come from Germany to establish itself on the north-east coast of England around the fifth century. This clinker-built coble has been acquired by the Harbour Commissioners as a link with the past as well as an attraction to holiday-makers.

Originally built in the town by brothers Baker and Percy Siddall for £75 in 1912, the vessel was named for the three sons of the owner, Mr Robert Crawford. It was powered by a simple lug sail and oars. This type of craft had a shallow draught with no keel, but had a very deep rudder, which was removed and used as a gangplank in the harbour.

Three Brothers had a unique design, allowing beam trawling as well as passenger carrying, with her less than normal sheer.

Joining *Three Brothers* is *Kate and Violet*, a 38ft. coble built on North Marine Drive, Flamborough, in 1911, by Mr. A. Hopwood for the Hutchinson family. She was used for five or six years for passenger service and local fishing before being motorised. Now fitted with a

38ft. mast of Scots spruce, she also has hand-made blocks for the running gear. She needs three and a half tons of ballast.

The Bridlington Sailing Coble Preservation Society exists to provide practical experience in sailing this type of craft and for this purpose the Society has defined a limited area of the Bay in which *Three Brothers* and *Kate and Violet* will sail.

The Society's patron is Lord Holderness and for a subscription of £3 p.a. individuals may join to preserve this fine example of an ancient vessel – a small cost to keep alive the tradition of locally built boats.

Baker, Percy and Jack – the boat-building Siddalls

It is almost impossible to look at the harbour in Bridlington or any postcard of Bridlington in the summer without seeing at least one craft built by one or more of a three-generation boat-building family of craftsmen.

The firm "Siddall & Son" was started about 1890 when the founder, Baker Siddall, who was born in Bridlington in 1864, turned his hand to boat-building. His father had been a ship's carpenter and had died at sea when Baker Siddall was a young boy. He had always been interested in boats and a model of a three-masted clipper which he made when he was a young teenager was presented to the Bridlington Council. It is now on show at the Museum in Sewerby Hall.

Soon after Baker started his business, he and his brother George, a master builder, built a workshop in Bow Street where it stands to this day.

Boat-building and boat repairing was not always a busy trade, especially during the summer months and, to supplement his business, Baker built himself a fleet of rowing boats and hired them out from the north beach at Bridlington.

Baker Siddall was to be joined by his son Percy at the age of twelve and in due course by his grandson Jack Siddall. Both continued in the same pattern, boat-building in the winter and hiring out rowing boats in the summer.

During the boat-building season, the workshop was always a popular place for many a man or boy to spend an hour or so watching the boats take shape. In the early days before electricity was installed, the work was carried out in lamp-light and candle-light and everything was done by hand.

The types of boats varied both in size and shape and these included Yorkshire cobles, which incidentally cost around £90 in the early 1900s, ferry boats, motor boats, rowing boats, salmon boats and many others.

All the rowing boats were clinker built and the planks were steamed ready for bending in a specially built long steaming box. A bill of sale still exists for Mr Fred Smith of Slipway for six rowing boats for £30 in 1892.

There were never any plans to work to, except for a few measurements scribbled on the back of a cigarette packet – all three generations relied on the keenness of their eye for the shape, and as each boat was finished a mark would be scratched on the wall of the workshop. Well over 500 marks have appeared over the years.

The wood used was always of the very best quality and often chosen whilst the tree was still growing in Boynton Woods, felled and planked and then stacked in slats outside Bow Street workshop to season for many months before use.

Some of the cobles built included *Frances Silver Line, My Judith, Elsie May, Lily, Three Bs Mon Plaisir* and *Three Brothers*, which has recently been restored to her former glory complete with sails and is now back in Bridlington harbour.

Rowing boats were built for Sid ("Yank") Tallentire, Fred Smith and his son Spodge, "Jean" Martin, Ted Newby and many many more. Many were also sold and used at other seaside and lakeside areas. It is said that when a rowing boat was built for Filey, Baker and Percy would row it there – this was before transport was available.

During the first world war, Percy Siddall joined the Royal Navy and twice the ship in

which he served was torpedoed and he was rescued. Baker meanwhile went to sea in a trawler. A rule was made that each trawler must carry a tender and for this purpose Baker built a suitable boat in one weekend. It was named *Felicity* and was to be used in the harbour for very many years. Jack Siddall served for six years in the Royal Navy during the

second world war and was minesweeping prior to the D-Day landings.

Generations of holidaymakers used to re-appear each summer to hire out the rowing boats or have a penny ride in *Selby Abbey* – the penny-rider boat. The fleet of boats were rowed onto to the north beach each day and rowed back to the harbour later, often in a south easterly gale. Over the years scores of young boys, including several of Percy Siddall's grandsons, acted as boatlads and they would bring in the boats to the wooden stages ready for people to embark and they would help to moor up back in the harbour and for this they would receive pocket money.

Sadly the boatbuilding and hiring firm came to an end in 1972 on the death of Jack Siddall, but looking into Bridlington Harbour the life's work of three generations of the local boat-building firm will live on for many years to come, and will give pleasure and a living to many more people.

There are a couple of young joiners still in the Siddall family and, who knows, one day as with Baker one might turn his hand to the family trade. At least the workshop and the old tools are still around.

Left, *Three Brothers* on a peaceful August after-noon, while, below, she races across Bridlington Bay on a blustery outing in June 1995.

1104 Marine Craft Unit

The 1104 Marine Craft Unit, Royal Air Force, came to Bridlington in 1932 to support the bombing range at Skipsea. In 1935 there were berths for eight armoured vessels. During the war, boats from Bridlington rescued 30 airmen.

Aircraftsman Shaw (Lawrence of Arabia) was in Bridlington in the 30s. He was sent here to carry out trials with a new power boat he helped to design and develop.

During the war, the unit became engaged in air-sea rescue and saved the lives of many aircrew forced to leave their bombers.

The armoured boats were also used to test new bomb sights later used to good effect in the war.

The unit become redundant when heli-copters came to Leconfield and it was disbanded on 8th December 1980.

Top: R.A.F. rescue boat 1386 at low tide in the harbour in 1961, and bottom, a group of R.A.F. boats moored in the harbour.

The Royal Yorkshire Yacht Club

The Royal Yorkshire Yacht Club has had a close association with Bridlington and its harbour for many years.

Records of the Club itself go back to May 1847, but it was probably in existence before that date. The first HQ was in a front room at the Victoria Hotel, Hull, overlooking the Humber. At first there were offices in both Hull and Whitby, but gradually the Club moved to Hull. Queen Victoria was the Club's first patron.

At the end of the century, the Club looked for an alternate sailing area as the extension of Hull docks made the Humber less attractive for yachting.

Records for the Club between 1860 and 1906 were lost when the Humber overflowed in December 1921. The cellars at Bowlalley Lane, where the records were kept, were flooded.

The RYYC took over the premises of Bridlington YC and continued to occupy them until 1938. Formerly the Ozone Hotel, at the junction of West Street and Windsor Crescent, the new clubhouse was purchased and altered at a cost of £6,500. The day fixed for removal to the new premises was Tuesday, 16th May 1938.

Since then the Club has celebrated its centenary and in 1997 celebrates 150 years of sailing.

With the exception of two world wars, a regatta has been held annually in Bridlington Bay, which attracts boats and sailors from yacht clubs around the country. In 1995 the RYYC held its 138th annual event.

The picture above shows *Jitterbug* leaving harbour, while below one of the majestic yachts of yesteryear races across the Bay.

Yachting at Bridlington.

Jet Boat Rides!

High-speed thrills are available by taking a trip on one of the two speedboats operating from Bridlington Harbour. Both local speedboats are built on 27ft. Powercraft hulls and are powered by 350hp turbocharged diesel engines manufactured by Sabre Marine Engines. These engines drive a jet unit of Italian manufacture and allow the boat to achieve 45mph. The hulls for these speedboats were chosen because they hold the British speed record for their type. They are specially strengthened to withstand the rigours of the North Sea. When running at full speed, the engines use between 10 and 15 gallons of fuel per hour. They have a life span in the arduous local conditions of three to four years. The hulls are run for six to seven years before replacement and both engines and hulls have to be constantly maintained to a high standard. The drivers of the speedboats have years of experience and are the envy of many of the passengers. For 1996, *Mirage* joins *Shockwave* for high-speed thrills in Bridlington Bay.

Bottom: *Shockwave* at speed in June 1995. Top: *Thunderbird* enters the harbour and (centre) *Splashdown* which operated in the late 80s. In the early 90s, *Terminator* was on duty, while during the 60s a speedboat named *007* was at work. Two high-speed former RAF launches were converted to *Bluebird* and *Swift* which operated in the 50s.

Bridlington's lifeboat service

The lifeboats at Bridlington, while not actually berthed in the harbour, must surely rate as an integral part of the story of the seafaring life of Bridlington Quay.

This volume cannot do justice to the history of the lifeboats in Bridlington and the subject is well documented in Mr. Ralph S. Fawcett's book, "The Bridlington Life-Boats."

The local lifeboat is housed about a quarter of a mile from the sea in purpose-built accommodation on South Marine Drive. Its location necessitates the transportation of the craft

along a much-used road to the launch slipway. A 17.5-tonne Talus MBH 200hp diesel-engined tractor with a top speed of 9mph takes only a few minutes to make the trip.

The current lifeboat at Bridlington is the *Marine Engineer* while its predecessor was the *Peggy and Alex Caird*, both Mersey class.

A 16ft D class inshore lifeboat is housed on the seafront a matter of yards from the south beach. This is the 20-knot inflatable *The Lords Feoffees* and this has been involved in 646 launches, saving 944 lives, since it arrived on 10th February 1984 having cost £6,000.

Briefly there have been 15 lifeboats at the Quay, the first serving from 1806 to 1824.

In 1806, townspeople of the Quay raised £300 for a boat and boathouse, the boat being built by Henry Greathead, the builder of the *Original*, the first lifeboat.

At this time, there were two lifeboats in the town. The national lifeboat house was at the junction of Chapel Street and the Promenade, while the fishermen's boat, the *Seagull*, was housed in the Sailors' and Workingmen's Club on Prince Street.

This first vessel, *Robert Whitworth*, served but a year with no service launches. A second *Robert Whitworth* had 16 lives to her credit while *John Abbott*, which served the town for 14 years, had two lives to hers. Records for both *Harbinger* and *Seagull* are not complete and lives saved by them are not known. The *Harbinger* was destroyed during the Great Gale and six crew were lost. *Seagull* was withdrawn after damage sustained in the disaster that claimed the life of Kit Brown, a local lifeboat medal winner.

William John and Frances saved 44 lives between 1885 and 1898, while the following year *George and Jane Walker* had no lives saved to her credit. The following year, a second boat arrived, named *George and Jane Walker* which served for 32 years. She had a total of 50 lives saved in 58 launches. Propelled by sail and oar, being launched from Trinity Cut, she was the last to be launched by horses, in 1920.

In more recent times, *Stanhope Smart* was launched in service 60 times with 53 lives saved. She served from June 1931 to November 1947, when *Tillie Morrison, Sheffield*, became the town's lifeboat. *Tillie Morrison* was a light self-righting boat 35ft. 6in. long, weighing less than seven tons. Her twin-screw 18hp twin engines could run even through the engine room was completely flooded. Her top speed was just over seven knots. She was named on 8th May 1938.

Although launched 23 times, *Tillie Morrison* is credited with no lives saved. After damage sustained when she overturned at Thornwick Bay during the summer of 1952 with the loss of Mr Robert

Above: The *William Henry and Mary King* was Bridlington's lifeboat between 1967 and 1988. She was of the Oakley class, 37ft long, with a beam of 11ft 6in. Her total weight, including crew and gear, was 12.45 tons. Built in 1964, she cost £33,000, and had a top speed of 8.16 knots, while her cruising speed was seven knots. This lifeboat was the only lifeboat not to display her number as she was the thirteenth in her class.

Below: Bridlington's recent lifeboat *Peggy and Alex Caird*, the first of her class, 12-001, who commenced duty in late 1989. The Mersey class lifeboats have a watertight wheelhouse which enables them to self-right in only six seconds. There is seating for six crew and a jump seat for a doctor. They are powered by two 285hp Caterpillar 3208T turbo-charged marine diesels which allow a cruising speed of 15.75 knots with top speed of 17 knots. *Peggy and Alex Caird* has an aluminium hull.

Above: *William Henry & Mary King* is launched in July 1978.

Centre: *RNLB Marine Engineer* and *Peggy and Alex Caird* on the south beach on change-over day, 13th August, 1995.

Below: *George and Jane Walker* enters the water assisted by a team of horses.

Redhead, she was temporarily replaced by the St. Abbs life-boat *Annie Ronald and Isabella Forrest*.

Tillie Morrison, Sheffield II, between June 1953 and 1967, saved 36 lives in her 106 service launches. Her first service was on 11th July 1953 when she went to assist the motorboat *Firefly*, driven ashore through waves breaking over her side and swamping the engine.

Before arriving at Bridlington she was on display at Derby for ten days. Built and named at Cowes, she sailed up the Trent to

RNLB Marine Engineer, with Coxswain Fred Walkington at the helm, is pictured below during a practice launch in June 1995 when she was the replacement vessel during repairs to *Peggy and Alex Caird*. During July of that year, *Marine Engineer* was placed on permanent station duties at Bridlington, while *Peggy and Alex Caird* was transferred to standby duties. *Marine Engineer* is the 12th of the Mersey class to be built and they are 11.57m long, beam 3.81m, draught .95m with a depth of 1.86m. The displacement is 13.85 tonnes. Fuel tanks hold approximately 245 gallons, to give a range of 145 nautical miles. *Marine Engineer*'s hull is of fibre reinforced composite.

Nottingham and then transported to Derby.

After *Tillie Morrison, William Henry and Mary King* was on station in the town until late 1988.

The *Peggy and Alex Caird*, a Mersey class lifeboat, was numbered 12-001, denoting she was 12m long and number one of her type. She came to Bridlington on 15th December 1988 and her first service was on 15th January 1989.

On Sunday, 13th August 1995, there was an official change-over of duties between the *Peggy and Alex Caird* and *Marine Engineer*.

Mr. Fred Walkington is the lifeboat coxswain with many years at the helm and he has gained a Bronze Medal.

The Bridlington Lifeboat

Launches and Rescues since records kept

	Launched	Lives Saved
Bridlington Lifeboat	712	394
Bridlington Inshore	646	944
To end of 1994		
1995		
Bridlington Lifeboat	12	5
Bridlington Inshore	19	8
Up to 12th August 1995		

Above: During June 1995, the 37m twin masted Dutch sailing ship *De Tukker* stayed overnight. Every year, *De Tukker* provides sailing experience to crews of young offenders from the Gateshead area. Seasickness and unfavourable winds during the North Sea crossing from Holland forced her to make for Hull. She visited Bridlington before going on to Gateshead.

Below: Two tugs from Holyhead Towing were in the harbour for the summer of 1995. The vessels, *Afon Lass* and *Afon Wen*, started their stay in the first week of July. Over a period of some months, the tugs were engaged in towing work on sea defences near Withernsea. The work consisted of towing a huge stone-carrying barge to the beach. The stone came from Norway in a barge capable of carrying 10,000 tons. The Holyhead tugs were required to take over the towing of the barge to the beach from three miles out. The weather had to be perfect or the barge could have broken in two because of its size. There was a crew of three for each boat, and there was a crew member on board at all times. The tugs were powered by Caterpillar engines of approx. 1000hp.

Private Boats for Fishing Parties

Fishing parties and individual anglers can fish from several boats provided by local fishermen and boat owners. Among this small fleet are traditional cobles and modern launches. All vessels carry approved Department of Transport life-saving equipment and are fully licensed for passenger carrying. The boatman provides tackle and bait if required. The vessels leave the harbour at various times dependent on tide and weather conditions, but during the summer times usually are 6.30am, 9.30am, 1.30pm and 6pm. The vessels operate off Flamborough Head mainly for cod, haddock, ling, plaice and skate. The length of trip varies but can be from two or three hours to six or more, but parties can arrange for trips of any duration. There are four shops close to the harbour which both hire and sell all fishing gear required.

In the table below, each vessel name gives number of anglers and a Bridlington (01262) contact number.

Vessel	Anglers	Contact	Vessel	Anglers	Contact
Rachel K	40	671723	Kimberley	12	08312 268898
Liberty	12-36	679002/678281	My Sharon	12	679434
Chance	36	676551	Teresa of Sark	12	675663
Seajay	36	673886	Aqua Star	12	671489
Eva Ann	36	676597	Silver Line	12	850047
Friends	12	602794/604643	Our Freda	12	677530
Yorkshire Lass	12	674954	Heidi J	12	605855
Sportsman	12	679915	Boy's Own	12	609119
Amaka Rose	12	671476			

Fishing Vessels under 13 metres in length

Reg. No.	Name	Built	Weight	Length	Breadth
H467	Amaka Rose	1978	9.06	11.90	3.69
SH156	Aqua Star	1989	6.41	11.12	3.72
H72	Chance	1982	11.92	12.00	3.81
CS65	Eva Ann	1971	12.81	12.19	3.44
H470	Friends	1978	5.91	10.43	3.51
SH235	Yorkshire Lass	1958	5.91	11.20	3.54
H131	Kimberley	1989	9.35	12.15	3.70
H86	My Charon	1980	8.17	11.60	4.00
	Our Freda	1913	13.15	11.77	3.20
H544	Heidi J	1980	9.52	10.67	3.84
H395	Tristar	1990	6.82	10.00	3.35

Fishing Vessels in Bridlington – the old and the new

In a photograph from the early Sixties, GY36 *Guiding Light* enters a placid habour, while below, H6 *Charlotte May* leaves on an extended fishing trip during July 1995. Note that in the picture above there is no cover for the crew working on deck, while in the modern vessel the working area is enclosed.

Bridlington's Fishing Industry

The fishing industry in Bridlington has suffered somewhat of a decline since the Common Fishing Policy failed to give the promised prosperity and stability.

There are severe catching restrictions and until fish stocks improve there seems to be no sign of an upsurge in the local industry.

There are four main methods of fishing from the port, which have been in use since the late 19th century: trawling, drift net, long line and potting.

Trawling takes place from March to October, and about 27 keel boats still fish from Bridlington. The trawlers land cod, haddock, whiting and plaice. Cobles also fish for cod, salmon, sea trout, lobsters and crabs.

Drift net fishing is used for herring, and long line fishing, usually for cod, takes place October to March.

Potting, between March and June, is for crabs and lobsters.

Sailing boats were originally used for fishing, larger vessels journeying out of the bay, but smaller cobles fished within the bay. After engines were introduced to sailing vessels about the time of the first world war, purpose-built boats were used.

Around 1912 there were 80 vessels operating from the harbour and over 150 men employed. In the late twenties numbers were down, but they increased after the Second World War. In 1969, 41 boats, 34 of them keel boats, were in use manned by about 150 men.

Nowadays, new technology in navigation, fish detection and catching are used, as well as storage facilities so that catches arrive in Bridlington in good condition.

About 20 years ago fishermen could sail two hours and catch enough fish for a living but these areas won't sustain a fleet all year round and skippers have to find other areas.

Left: FR28 *Ocean Reward* is accompanied by the ever-present seagulls as she heads into harbour. This vessel was built at Fraserburgh in 1969, with a blue wooden hull 16.58 metres in length weighing 24.78 tons. She is powered by a 310hp Gardner engine.

One of the impressive vessels to be seen in Bridlington harbour is SH76 *Wayfinder*, a stern trawler.

Owned by Mr Peter Ibbotson and Mr Robert Ibbotson, she was bought in France where she had been called *Arpeage*. She has a crew of six, including the brother owners, and makes a fine sight in the harbour with her orange and white livery.

When built in 1976 she was 21.12 metres long with a gross weight of 82 tons. She had a wooden hull and powered by a 589hp Baudouin engine.

In 1986, she was refitted at Grimsby, including the installation of a new engine.

The picture below shows the bright orange and white *Wayfinder* towering over *Lagernoon* while at rest in the harbour at Bridlington.

Above: INS279 *Margaret H* at rest, while on the right, she takes nets on board.

Below: *Margaret H* high and dry at low tide alongside Harbour Road. She was built in 1980 at Lossiemouth, weighs over 47 tons and is 17.5m long. Her hull is painted deep blue.

Right: *Ubique*'s crew unloads the catch, assisted by the driver of the Toyota fork-lift truck.

Centre right: Fish boxes are loaded onto *Industry* in the afternoon sunlight.

Bottom right: Ice is tipped onto the deck of *Tradition*.

Some boats have their own named plastic containers and loaded with the silvery harvest they are lifted from the fish hold by a system of ropes and pulleys. The hooks are placed to lift the cases and the signal given to hoist. The crewman wraps a rope around the winch and the catch is lifted out into the open. The load is pivoted to the side of the quay where it is placed on a pallet. When a dozen or so boxes are ready a forklift truck transfers this load to the articulated lorries waiting nearby. The lorries are despatched to Hull where the catch is sold.

After being emptied, the boats then receive a consignment of ice. The ice is stored in a 35-ton silo and the forklift trucks take a skip containing half a ton to the ship's side and dumps it on the deck. The crew then shovel it below deck. A half-ton load takes two hours to make in the ice machine plant and only a couple of minutes to discharge into the skip.

After taking on ice, empty fish containers are loaded. Boats are refuelled and reprovisioned, then move away to be moored away from the fish quay.

As there may be as many as half a dozen trawlers being unloaded, iced, reloaded and manoeuvred simultaneously, it was necessary to allow work to continue unhindered by the watching tourists.

The fish quay building has incorporated in it a viewing platform so that the whole operation can be watched in comfort.

The changing appearance of *Galatea* is shown in these two images of the same vessel. In the top picture, PD53 *Galatea* is tied up alongside south pier some time in the late 80s. Built in 1975 at Bideford, she weighed 50 tons with a length of just over 21m. This photograph was taken before her refit as H82 *Galatea C.* Her registered dimensions are now: Length 21.26m, breadth 6.42 m and depth 2.38m. Her registered tonnage is now 98.06. with a maximum service displacement of 183.38 tonnes. She is painted bright red and white, and makes an impressive sight as she leaves harbour during August 1995 for one of her seven-day stints in the North Sea fishing grounds.

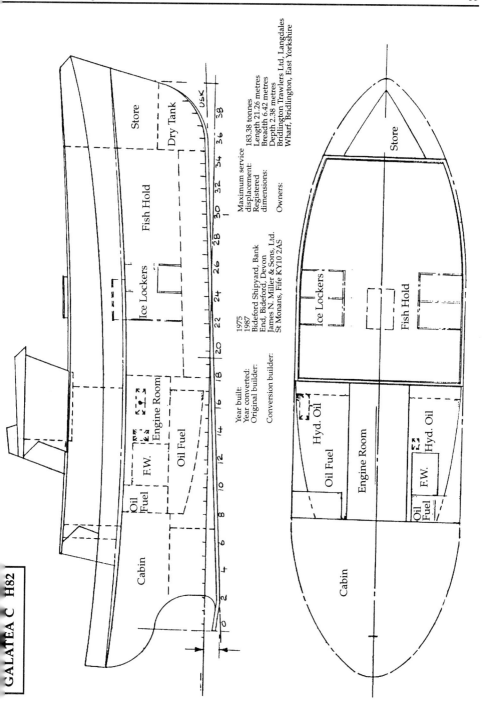

GALATEA C H82

Store

Dry Tank

Fish Hold

Ice Lockers

Engine Room

F.W.

Oil Fuel

Oil Fuel

Cabin

Store

Fish Hold

Ice Lockers

Hyd. Oil

Engine Room

Oil Fuel

F.W.

Hyd. Oil

Oil Fuel

Cabin

Year built: 1975
Year converted: 1987
Original builder: Bideford Shipyard, Bank
                               End, Bideford, Devon
Conversion builder: James N. Miller & Sons, Ltd.
                               St Monans, Fife KY10 2AS

Maximum service
displacement: 183.38 tonnes
Registered   Length 21.26 metres
dimensions: Breadth 6.42 metres
                               Depth 2.38 metres
Owners: Bridlington Trawlers Ltd, Langdales
                               Wharf, Bridlington, East Yorkshire

Above: OB24 *Moyallon* alongside *Crusader* with *Charlotte May* in the rear. *Moyallon* was built at Girvan, Ayrshire, in 1985, is 11.92m long with a gross tonnage of 18.24. Her wooden hull has a varnished finish.

Left: H484 *Pickering* tied up in the harbour after her fishing duties. She was built in 1975 in Cobh in Ireland, had a weight of 67+ tons and her wooden light blue hull was over 20m long. She had a 350hp Cummins engine.

In 1987, the Vicar of Sewerby exorcised "a restless spirit" from the vessel. A former skipper, Michael Laws, said a previous owner had seen a ghostly figure with a flat cap in the middle of the night.

Skipper Gates and his crew experienced odd occurrences on board, including the steering, which would drive the ship round in circles, and every morning the radar system went haywire. The engine also kept breaking down.

It was discovered that in the past a man on the vessel had been lost over board. After the exorcism service the vessel has provided some successful fishing trips, and there was a completely different atmosphere aboard the vessel.

Left: H482 *St Leger* framed by the unloading winch as she rests alongside the fish dock of south pier. She was built at Paull in 1978, has a length of 17.8 metres and weighs 32 tons. Her bottle green steel hull measures 5.65m in width and she has a draught of 2.21m. Her motive power was provided by a 394hp Baudouin engine.

Below: GY1375 *Grenaa Way* approaches the entrance to Bridlington Harbour. This vessel was built in Denmark in 1966, weighed over 49 tons, her length was 18m, width 5.3m and draught 2.48m. Her light blue wooden hull, built oak on oak, had a cruiser stern and was powered by a 270hp Scania D11 engine. In August 1995, she was advertised in *Fishing News* for sale at £18,000, her fishing gear having been removed.

Left: PD192 *Contester* is overtaken by the speedboat as she makes her way into the harbour. A Peterhead boat built in 1967, she is a 35-ton wooden vessel 18m in length with red-painted hull.

Above: Head-on view of SH173 *Crusader* as she heads for the harbour entrance. *Crusader* is a 32-ton wooden vessel built in 1969 at Seahouses. She has a 200hp Gardner engine and is 18m long.

Left: With a blue hull, H256 *Radiant Trust* was built in 1972 at Stromness in the Orkneys, weighing 27+ tons with a length of 16.77m.

Right: H132 *Silverwood* tied up alongside LH157 *Success II* at the landward end of the Chicken Run in the late 80s. Note that the rebuilding of the repair facility has not been carried out. *Success II* was built in 1949 at St Monans. A 172hp Gardner engine powered her wooden cruiser-stern hull, which was 16.2m long, 5.3m wide and 24+ tons in weight. Her green hull contrasts well with the bright red of *Silverwood*.

Below: MR1 *Innovator* celebrates Bridlington's 1994 August Harbour Gala as she takes part in the review. *Innovator* arrived in Bridlington only a week previously. She was built in Hull in 1993, is all but 14m long weighing over 26 tons. Her red hull is topped by white superstructure. She is the first vessel to be registered at Manchester.

Above: H170 *Dominant* heads
for the calm waters of
Bridlington harbour on a fine
sunny day. *Dominant* is now
decommissioned. Built in 1962
in Holland, she was over 17m
long and weighed more than 22
tons. Her power was provided
by a 319hp Volvo Penta engine.
She had a black hull.

Right: H105 *Excelsior* enters the
harbour at low tide.

Right: SH65 *Laura Eve*
alongside south pier in the late
80s. She had white
superstructure and a light blue
hull.

Right: GY315 *Sea Venture* heads for the unloading area on the south pier, her crew ready for action. *Sea Venture* is now decommissioned. Built in Sweden in 1947, she weighed 27 tons, was 17.6m long, 5m wide with a black wooden hull powered by a 320hp Volvo Penta engine.

Below: PW82 *Atlanta II* interests several onlookers as she enters the harbour in her white livery with blue and red stripes. Built in 1987 at Mevagissey, Cornwall, she is 11.75m long and over 21 tons in weight.

Above: SH165 *Onward Star* gets a new coat of deep blue paint alongside the harbour wall outside the Harbourmaster's Office. Powered by a 320hp Volvo Penta engine, her cruiser-sterned hull is 16m long. She weighs over 39 tons and is 5.39m wide. Built in 1966 at Fraserburgh.

Below: GY92 *Eagernoon* thrust her way into the placid harbou waters of Bridlington on a fin spring day. She has a steel hul painted maroor

Above: SH173 *Crusader* moves to her mooring against a background of the walkway.
Below: H12 *Three Fevers IV* enters the harbour during early August 1995. She is dark blue with white superstructure.

Left: H18 *St. Andrew* is nearly home in the evening sunlight. A Danish-built vessel, she was completed in 1963, weighing over 47 tons, and her cruiser-sterned hull is over 18m long and 5.6m wide. She is powered by a 268hp Scania engine. When photographed she was light blue, but in mid-1995 was bright red.

Below: KY28 *Ubique* in the harbour on a fine sunny day. Powered by a 270hp Volvo Penta engine, *Ubique* was built at St Monans in 1974. She has a transom stern to her red wooden hull, and she weighs 24+ tons, is 16.8m in length and 5.2m in width.

Right: H273 *Regal
Star* leaves
Bridlington
Harbour on a fine
sunny afternoon.
She has a light
blue hull.

elow: SY86 *Diana*
ɪ the evening
ɪnlight as she is
ɔout to pass the
ɪd of north pier.
ɪnother vessel
uilt in the
ɪrkneys at
ɪromness, in 1971,
iana weighs over
ƨ tons, is 16.6m
ng and 5.6m
ʿide. She has a
ɪnsom stern with
ɪream wooden
ɪll powered by a
ǀ4hp Volvo Penta
ɪgine.

PORT REGISTRATION CODES

Port Registration Codes seen on fishing vessels in Bridlington Harbour

A	=	Aberdeen	LH	=	Leith
AH	=	Abroath	LK	=	Lerwick
AR	=	Ayr	LT	=	Lowestoft
BA	=	Ballantrae	M	=	Milford Haven
BCK	=	Buckie	MR	=	Manchester
BF	=	Banff	PD	=	Peterhead
BM	=	Brixham	PW	=	Padstow
FD	=	Fleetwood	SH	=	Scarborough
FR	=	Fraserburg	SN	=	North Shields
GY	=	Grimsby	SY	=	Stornaway
H	=	Hull	WH	=	Weymouth
INS	=	Inverness	WK	=	Wick
K	=	Kirkwall	WY	=	Whitby
KY	=	Kirkcaldy			

Below: H103 *Three Fevers III* approaches the harbour entrance with crew members waiting on deck. *Three Fevers III* is a liner, built in 1947 at St Monans, and weighs 22 tons, with a wooden hull. She is 16.3m long, 5.1m wide and is powered by a Gardner engine.

Right: H20 *Acorn*, a wooden 25-ton vessel, moves away from the south pier before making her way to her moorings. She was first registered as KY133, built in 1956, at Cellardyke, Fifeshire, and she was sold to Broadford, Isle of Skye. She came to Bridlington in 1963 when re-registered as BRD32. Common Market regulations produced another registration, H20, and the vessel left Bridlington when the owners took over *Laura Eve*. When pictured, *Acorn*'s hull was painted light blue.

Below: H443 *Industry* manoevres away from the south pier on a fine late afternoon. A 1967-built vessel, *Industry* is powered by a 310hp Gardner engine. She has a wooden hull with a cruiser stern, weighing 36+ tons. Her length is 16.3m, being 5.54m wide, with a 2.16m draught. *Industry* has a light blue hull.

Left: H87
My Rose Anne approaches the entrance to the harbour. She is a product of the John Harker Shipyards at Knottingley, built there in 1969. Her 310hp Gardner engine powers a red steel hull with cruiser stern, she weighs 40 tons, with a length of 16.3m, 5.2m width, and a draught of 2.09m.

Below: H232 *Tradition* nears the harbour with a background of South Marine Drive. With a wooden hull and transom stern, *Tradition* is powered by a 310hp Volvo Penta engine. She is painted light blue, weighs 24+ tons, is 13.6m long, her width 4.97m and draught 1.92m.

Above: H58 *Christel Star* approaching the south pier after a fishing trip. She has a dark blue wooden hull, 12m long, and was built in 1983 at Hull.

Left: FR38 *Pamela S* high and dry against Harbour Road. A Fraserburgh-built vessel, *Pamela S* weighs 24+ tons, is 16.9m long, 5.58m wide and her deep blue wooden cruiser-sterned hull, built in 1969, is powered by a 310hp Gardner engine.

Below: H446 *Sarb-J* was wrecked off Robin Hoods Bay in the early 1990s. She was built in 1977 at Knottingley with a 375hp Kelvin engine. Her black steel hull weighed 29+ tons, was 17.9m long, 5.61m wide with a draught of 2.06m.

Left: SH163 *Mary Allison* is pictured alongside the chicken run, against a backdrop of a crowded south pier. She is a wooden vessel, built at Scarborough in 1968. She weighs 44 tons and is 17m long. At the time she was photographed, *Mary Allison* was painted yellow.

After the 1914-18 war, many Scottish herring drifters visited Bridlington. Sometimes it was possible to walk from South Pier to Crane Wharf without touching water. Scottish girls came with the boats to clean and gut the herrings on land at the west end of the harbour. The fish was then barrelled and sent inland for sale.

Below: SH52 *Silver Line* makes her way past the end of north pier before turning into the harbour entrance. Built in Arbroath in 1977, she weighs 25 tons and is 17m long. *Silver Line* was painted white, dark blue and light blue when photographed.

Above: FR408 *Enchanter* in the peaceful waters of Bridlington harbour on a fine June evening. This trawler is powered by a 230hp Gardner engine, has a blue wooden hull with a cruiser stern. She weighs 23+ tons, is 16.8m long, 5.36m wide, with a draught of 1.8m.

Hand-drawn sign on south pier at Bridlington during August 1995.

Right:
H491 *Janet M* approaches the harbour on an August evening. *Janet M* was built in Hull in 1979 with a 300hp Cummins power plant. She has a blue steel hull with transom stern and weighs 23+ tons, with a length of 15.3m, width 4.88m and a draught of 1.95m.

Above: With crew members on deck, H340 *St Keverne* eases her way round the canch and makes for the harbour entrance. *St Keverne* has a steel, transom-sterned hull painted black, is powered by a 390hp Baudouin engine, is 32+ tons, and her main dimensions are 17.72m long 5.66m wide, 2.21m draught.

Below: GY1388 *Sunningdale* heads into harbour after unloading at south pier. Painted black, *Sunningdale*, now scrapped, was built in Holland in 1950, 15m in length weighing 17 tons.

Above: M38 *Castle Bay* huddles against the south pier. Built in 1985 at Neyland, M38 was originally named *Castle Bay of Dale*, and is 11.78m long weighing 21.61 tons. This vessel is painted bright red.

Right: SH68 *Incentive* tied up in the harbour. She weighs 17.85 tons, her black hull is 12.42m long and she was built in Fraserburgh.

Below: FR 408 *Enchanter* has the final touches put to her name during June 1995.

Left: FR68 *Betty* eases off the power to negotiate the entrance to the harbour. One of the many local Fraserburgh-built vessels, *Betty* had a 152hp Gardner engine powering her cruiser-sterned black wooden hull. She was built in 1960, weighing 23+ tons, 15.85m long, 5.27m wide with a draught of 1.82m. *Betty* left Bridlington harbour at midnight on 28th November, 1995, sailing for Grimsby, where she was scrapped.

Below: H45 *Pilot Us* passes the end of Crane Wharf on her way through the harbour. She was built in 1969 at Fraserburgh, is of wooden construction weighing 42 tons with a length of 15m. Her hull is painted red.

Above: INS 279 *Margaret H* rests alongside south pier on a fine June morning. She is powered by a Kelvin engine. Below: It seems the whole fishing fleet is at home. Left to right: PZ576 *Boy Gary*, H1051 *Josie B*, H273 *Regal Star* and SD101 *Katie Jane*.

Above: The *Charlotte May*, H6, arrived in the harbour on 15th July 1987, completing her maiden voyage from the St Monans, Fife, boatyard where she was built, costing £500,000.

The 20m high-tech trawler was skippered by her owner, Harvey Holbrook, the vessel being named after Mr Holbrook's mother and grandmother. Mr Holbrook handed his other boat *Margaret H*, to his son, David, and auctioned for charity the first box of fish landed after the first trip in the new vessel, keeping up an old harbour tradition. She has a 650hp engine.

The larger vessels of Bridlington's fishing fleet, of which *Charlotte May* is one, are able to work about 200 miles or so out to sea and stay away over a week at a time.

Below: SU345 *Telesis* forces her way through the water as she is about to enter the harbour.

Above: WH480 *Lia-G* nestles between FR68 *Betty* and SH163 *Mary Allison* alongside south pier. *Lia-G* is Portsmouth-built with a Baudouin power plant. She has a steel hull and weighs 24+ tons. She is 15.24m long with a width of 5m and a 1.82m draught.

Below: SU116 *Galwad-y-Mor*, built in 1986 at Polruan, Cornwall. She is 11.95m in length and weighs 31.5 tons gross. She is striped medium blue, black, light blue, white and brown.

Above: *Orion* enters harbour during
August 1995.

Above: The crew of WY306 *Harvester* on the deck
as they near the south pier. *Harvester* is painted
bright orange.

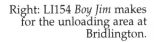

Right: H1051 *Josie B* makes her
entrance to the harbour on an
August day in 1995.

Right: LI154 *Boy Jim* makes
for the unloading area at
Bridlington.

*Reproductions of
photographs in this volume
are available. Contact the
author for details*

Can you believe it?

The Bridlington fishing fleet provided nearly £1,500,000 worth of food in 1976 and gave employment to over 500 local men.

Can you believe it?

In 1987 Bridlington was the seventh largest fishing port in England and Wales.

Above: OB280 *Challenge* approaches the unloading area on the south pier at Bridlington.

Left: The crew of *Challenge* unloads the catch with the aid of the winch.

Challenge was built in 1958 at the Macduff shipyards. She has a dark blue wooden hull with transom stern. He is powered by a 150hp Gardner engine, she weighs 23+ tons, is 15.5m long, 4.63m wide and has a draught of 1.9m.

Right: A catch of shellfish awaits the forklift before being loaded in the lorry for delivery.

Bridlington Harbour

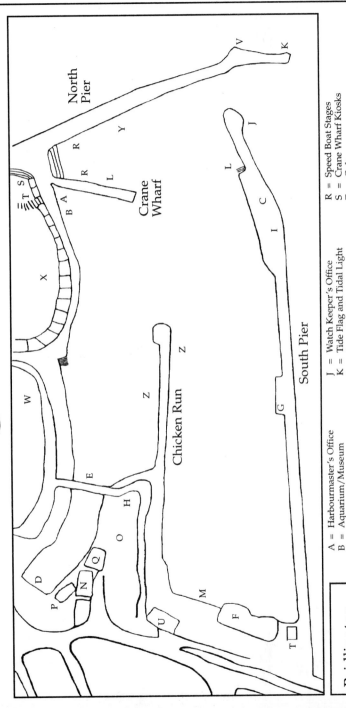

Bridlington Harbour: The Key

A = Harbourmaster's Office
B = Aquarium/Museum
C = Fish Quay
D = Clough Hole and Gypsey Race
E = Site of former Footbridge
F = The Lawrence Complex
G = Crane
H = Walkway
I = Fish Merchants' Office
J = Watch Keeper's Office
K = Tide Flag and Tidal Light
L = Ferry Boat Steps
M = Gummers Landing
N = Bridlington Fishermen's Selling Co.
O = Langdale Wharf Car Park
P = Taste o' The Sea
Q = Bridlington Trawlers Ltd.
R = Speed Boat Stages
S = Crane Wharf Kiosks
T = Cafe
U = Harbour Commissioners Office
V = R.Y.Y.C. Starting Point
W = Gardens and Seating
X = Shopping Area
Y = Pleasure Boats
Z = Angling Cobles